ON

TOUCHSTONE

WORKBOOK 2B

MICHAEL MCCARTHY

JEANNE MCCARTEN

HELEN SANDIFORD

CAMBRIDGE
UNIVERSITY PRESS

CAMBRIDGE
UNIVERSITY PRESS

University Printing House, Cambridge CB2 8BS, United Kingdom

One Liberty Plaza, 20th Floor, New York, NY 10006, USA

477 Williamstown Road, Port Melbourne, VIC 3207, Australia

314–321, 3rd Floor, Plot 3, Splendor Forum, Jasola District Centre, New Delhi – 110025, India

103 Penang Road, #05-06/07, Visioncrest Commercial, Singapore 238467

Cambridge University Press is part of the University of Cambridge.

It furthers the University's mission by disseminating knowledge in the pursuit of education, learning, and research at the highest international levels of excellence.

www.cambridge.org
Information on this title: www.cambridge.org/9781107618619

First published 2005
Second Edition 2014

20 19 18 17 16 15 14 13 12 11 10 9 8 7 6 5

Printed in Great Britain by CPI Group (UK) Ltd, Croydon CR0 4YY

A catalog record for this publication is available from the British Library.

ISBN 978-1-107-68173-6 Student's Book
ISBN 978-1-107-68175-0 Student's Book A
ISBN 978-1-107-62704-8 Student's Book B
ISBN 978-1-107-69037-0 Workbook
ISBN 978-1-107-64988-0 Workbook A
ISBN 978-1-107-61861-9 Workbook B
ISBN 978-1-107-65940-7 Full Contact
ISBN 978-1-107-61439-0 Full Contact A
ISBN 978-1-107-66547-7 Full Contact B
ISBN 978-1-107-62402-3 Teacher's Edition with Assessment Audio CD/CD-ROM
ISBN 978-1-107-67757-9 Class Audio CDs (4)

Additional resources for this publication at www.cambridge.org/touchstone2

Contents

1 What are they going to do?

Grammar and vocabulary

A Match the sentences.

1. My friends are planning a trip to Ecuador. __d__
2. They're going to call a hotel near the airport. _____
3. They have to go to the bank. _____
4. They bought a guidebook. _____
5. They need to do some research. _____
6. They're going to the drugstore. _____

a. They wanted to learn more about the country.

b. They want to buy some travel-size toiletries.

c. They need to change some money.

✓d. They want to learn Spanish.

e. They want to find cheap flights.

f. They want to make a reservation for one night.

B Combine the sentences. Write one sentence for each pair of sentences in part A.

1. _My friends are going to go to Ecuador to learn Spanish._
2. _____
3. _____
4. _____
5. _____
6. _____

2 Reasons for getting away

Grammar | **Imagine you are going to Australia for a vacation. Write sentences using the cues given.**

1. We want to <u>*go to the Great Barrier Reef to learn to dive*</u> .
   (go to the Great Barrier Reef / learn to dive)

2. I'd like to _____ .
   (get tickets to the Sydney Opera House / see a concert)

3. We're going _____ .
   (fly to the outback / go walking)

4. I'd like _____ .
   (visit Tasmania / see some friends)

5. I need _____ .
   (go online / find some cheap hotels)

6. We want _____ .
   (go shopping / buy some opal jewelry)

3 Online forum

Grammar | **Complete the questions on the online forum. Then answer the questions with true information about your town or city.**

Visitor's Center Forum

1. **From:** clueless | *Is it important to bring a guidebook?* | (important / bring a guidebook)

   From: travelsmart | *Yes, it is, and it's also useful to bring a phrase book.*

2. **From:** nocreditcard | | (safe / carry cash)

   From: travelsmart |

3. **From:** walksalot | | (expensive / rent a car)

   From: travelsmart |

4. **From:** concernedtourist | | (easy / find cheap restaurants)

   From: travelsmart |

5. **From:** wiseowl | | (hard / get around)

   From: travelsmart |

6. **From:** advanceplanner | | (necessary / make hotel reservations)

   From: travelsmart |

1 What is it?

Vocabulary **A** Write the words under the pictures.

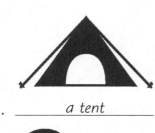

1. ___a tent___

2. _____

3. _____

4. _____

5. _____

6. _____

B Circle the correct words and complete the sentences.

1. When you go on a trip, you need to take a toothbrush and ___toothpaste___ to clean your teeth.
   a. soap
   b. a tent
   (c.) toothpaste

2. Use _____ at the beach to protect your skin.
   a. makeup
   b. sunscreen
   c. a pair of scissors

3. Don't forget to take _____ to wear in bed.
   a. pajamas
   b. a bathing suit
   c. sandals

4. Most hotels have _____ if you need to wash your hair.
   a. soap
   b. a brush
   c. shampoo

5. When you go camping, you need _____ so you can keep warm at night.
   a. insect repellent
   b. a flashlight
   c. a sleeping bag

6. Many hotels don't have _____ in the bathroom, so if you want to shave, you need to take one with you.
   a. a brush
   b. a razor
   c. a towel

7. Always take _____ on trips because you can get hurt or get sick.
   a. batteries
   b. a towel
   c. a first-aid kit

8. It's important to take _____ for your flashlight and your camera.
   a. batteries
   b. pajamas
   c. makeup

9. Wear _____ to keep your feet cool when it's hot.
   a. sunglasses
   b. sandals
   c. a hat

10. Always wear _____ if there are insects and mosquitoes.
    a. sunscreen
    b. makeup
    c. insect repellent

2 I think you should . . .

Grammar | Circle the correct words to complete the advice. Then add your own advice in the spaces below.

1. A We're going hiking in the mountains this weekend. What should we take?
   B Well, you should **to take** / (**take**) insect repellent and a first-aid kit.
   You want to wear good hiking boots, too.

2. A We're going skiing for the first time next month.
   B You know, it's easy to get a sunburn. **Don't forget** / **Why don't you** to use sunscreen.
   _____

3. A I want to go backpacking in Asia on my next vacation.
   B Then you need **pack** / **to pack** a lot of light clothes.
   _____

4. A My mother and I are planning a shopping trip in Hong Kong.
   B Then you really **could** / **should** take an empty suitcase with you.
   _____

5. A It's my friend's birthday on Friday. She's planning an all-night party.
   B In that case, **to take** / **take** your pajamas with you.
   _____

6. A I'm going on a camping trip, but I'm scared of the dark.
   B **Do you want** / **Why don't you** take a flashlight?
   _____

7. A I'm really excited about my trip to Paris. We're going to do a lot of walking.
   B You shouldn't **to forget** / **forget** to take some comfortable shoes then.
   _____

8. A I'm starting a dance class next week, but I don't have the right shoes.
   B You could **borrow** / **to borrow** your sister's shoes.
   _____

3 Travel suggestions

Grammar and vocabulary | Give some advice to a tourist on vacation in your country. Complete the sentences with your own ideas.

1. Don't forget _to pack a bathing suit_____ .
2. It's a good idea _____ .
3. You could _____ .
4. You shouldn't _____ .
5. Why don't you _____ .
6. You should _____ .

/ # That's a great idea.

1 Responding to suggestions

Conversation
strategies Who really likes each suggestion? Circle *a* or *b*.

1. Let's go out for sushi tomorrow.
   - a. That's a great idea.
   - b. I don't know. I don't really like fish.

2. We should go hiking together sometime.
   - a. I'd love to! When?
   - b. Maybe someday.

3. Why don't we get some tickets and see a show?
   - a. I don't know. Theater tickets are pretty expensive.
   - b. That sounds like fun. What do you want to see?

4. Would you like to go shopping for souvenirs this morning?
   - a. That sounds like a good idea. Where do you want to go?
   - b. Yeah, maybe we should do that sometime.

5. Let's drive through South America next summer.
   - a. I'd like to, but I need to get a part-time job.
   - b. That's an interesting idea. Let's do it.

2 That sounds great.

Conversation
strategies Write two responses to each suggestion. Write a response to show you like the suggestion. Then write a response to show you don't like it.

1. A Let's drive up to the mountains next weekend.

   B *That sounds great. When should we leave?*

   I don't know. It's pretty cold this time of year.

2. A We could take a semester off from school and go backpacking.

   B _____

   _____

3. A Why don't we go snorkeling sometime?

   B _____

   _____

4. A We should go camping next spring.

   B _____

   _____

5. A Why don't we just stay home, watch TV, and relax over the winter break?

   B _____

   _____

3 I guess . . .

Conversation strategies | Circle the correct use of *I guess*. There is only one in each sentence. Cross out the others.

1. Maria Would you like to go dancing tomorrow night?

   Nick I have to ~~I guess~~ work, but (I guess) I could go on Sunday night.

2. Lucy Why don't you come to the beach with me this weekend?

   Emi **I guess** I should get **I guess** away. But I should **I guess** study for my exams, **I guess**.

3. Tania Let's eat out tonight. I'd like to try that new Mexican restaurant downtown.

   Sylvia We could **I guess** try it, **I guess**, but I really **I guess** feel like Italian tonight.

4. Olivia I went to India last summer, and the food was amazing! I loved it!

   Chad Yeah, it's good. **I guess** I could **I guess** make some Indian food tonight.

5. Marc Mandy and I have four tickets to a Broadway show on Friday. You and Mari should come with us.

   Taka We could, **I guess**, but we don't **I guess** have a babysitter.

4 Let's see a movie.

Conversation strategies | Unscramble the suggestions. Write your own responses using *I guess*. Add more information.

1. tonight / Let's / after class / see a movie .
   Let's see a movie after class tonight.

   I guess we could. I don't have any plans.

2. drive / Why / to the beach / don't we ?

3. grandmother / visit / this weekend / Let's / my .

4. don't we / in the mountains / go camping / Why ?

5. could / We / a couple of weeks / for / to Europe / go .

6. want to / meet / Do / my / you / parents ?

1 A trip of a lifetime

Reading | **A** Read the article. Write the correct heading for each paragraph.

A Salt, Salt Everywhere   **B** A Place to Chill Out   **C** Dive into the Lobby

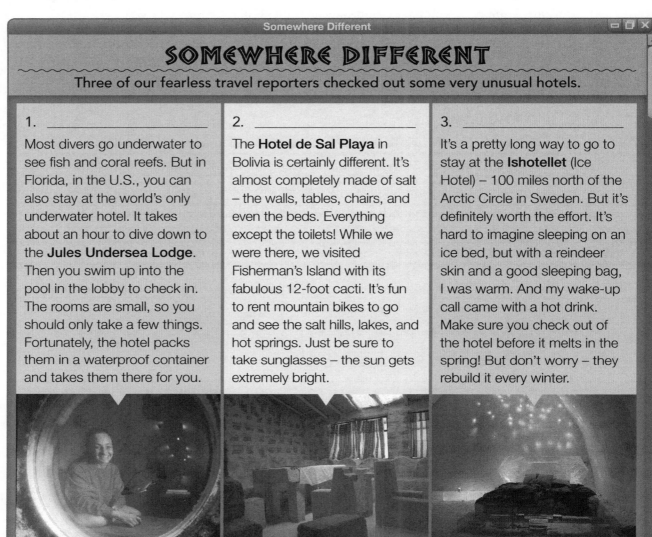

Somewhere Different

SOMEWHERE DIFFERENT

Three of our fearless travel reporters checked out some very unusual hotels.

1. _____

Most divers go underwater to see fish and coral reefs. But in Florida, in the U.S., you can also stay at the world's only underwater hotel. It takes about an hour to dive down to the **Jules Undersea Lodge**. Then you swim up into the pool in the lobby to check in. The rooms are small, so you should only take a few things. Fortunately, the hotel packs them in a waterproof container and takes them there for you.

2. _____

The **Hotel de Sal Playa** in Bolivia is certainly different. It's almost completely made of salt – the walls, tables, chairs, and even the beds. Everything except the toilets! While we were there, we visited Fisherman's Island with its fabulous 12-foot cacti. It's fun to rent mountain bikes to go and see the salt hills, lakes, and hot springs. Just be sure to take sunglasses – the sun gets extremely bright.

3. _____

It's a pretty long way to go to stay at the **Ishotellet** (Ice Hotel) – 100 miles north of the Arctic Circle in Sweden. But it's definitely worth the effort. It's hard to imagine sleeping on an ice bed, but with a reindeer skin and a good sleeping bag, I was warm. And my wake-up call came with a hot drink. Make sure you check out of the hotel before it melts in the spring! But don't worry – they rebuild it every winter.

B Read the article again. Find the information.

1. How do you get to the Jules Undersea Lodge?   _You dive underwater to get to it._

2. How long does it take to get to the Jules Undersea Lodge?   _____

3. What are three interesting things to see near the Hotel de Sal Playa?   _____

4. Why do you need sunglasses at the Hotel de Sal Playa?   _____

5. Where do you sleep at the Ice Hotel?   _____

6. Why do they have to rebuild the Ice Hotel every year?   _____

2 An email from Ireland

Writing | **A** Read Annie's email to Beth. Then match the email sections to the correct sentences.

- Say something you are going to do.
- Describe the place, food, or weather.
- End the email.
- Start the email. ———
- Say something you did.
- Say if you're enjoying your stay.
- Attach a photo and describe it.

New Message

To: B_Ohara@cup.com
Subject: **Greetings from the Emerald Isle**

Dear Beth,

I'm having a fabulous time here in Ireland.

We're staying in Baltimore, a beautiful fishing village. I'm attaching a photo so you can see all the fishermen's cottages.

Today we went kayaking and saw birds and seals.

Tomorrow our guide is taking us to an old castle. It's going to be a lot of fun.

See you next week!

Annie

B Write an email to a friend. Tell him or her about a place you visited once.

New Message

To:
Subject:

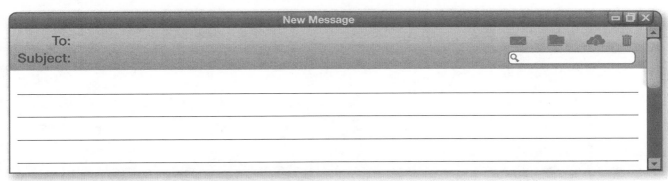

Unit 7 Progress chart

What can you do? Mark the boxes. ✓ = I can . . . ? = I need to review how to . . .	To review, go back to these pages in the Student's Book.
Grammar ☐ use infinitives to give reasons.	66 and 67
☐ use *It's* + adjective + *to* . . .	66 and 67
☐ ask for and give advice and suggestions.	69
Vocabulary ☐ name at least 5 things to do to get ready for a trip.	66 and 67
☐ name at least 12 things to pack for different kinds of trips.	68 and 69
Conversation strategies ☐ respond to suggestions I like and don't like.	70 and 71
☐ use *I guess* when I'm unsure about something.	71
Writing ☐ format and use correct expressions in an email.	73

At home

Lesson A — Spring cleaning

1 Whose is it?

Grammar and vocabulary

A Complete the chart with the correct pronouns.

Subject pronouns	Object pronouns	Possessive adjectives	Possessive pronouns
I	me		mine
you			
he		his	
she			
we			
they			

B Look at the pictures and write questions with *Whose*. Then answer the questions using possessive pronouns.

1. A *Whose suitcases are those?*
   B *They're ours.*

2. A _____
   B _____

3. A _____
   B _____

4. A _____
   B _____

5. A _____
   B _____

6. A _____
   B _____

2 After the party

Grammar | Circle the correct words to complete the conversation.

Karen   Wow! What a mess.

Matt   Are all of these things **our / (ours)**?

Karen   No, they're things people forgot when they left the party last night.

Matt   Well, I'm looking for **my / mine** jacket.

Karen   Is this **your / yours** jacket?

Matt   No, that's not **my / mine**. **My / Mine** is blue. I guess that's Felipe's.

Karen   No, it's not **him / his**. Felipe's jacket's gray.

Matt   Oh, well. Wow! Look at those DVDs. Whose are they?

Karen   I think they're your parents'. Yeah, these are **their / theirs**. We borrowed them when we were at **their / theirs** house last weekend.

Matt   Oh, yeah, . . . right. Hey, whose keys are these? Are they Jan's?

Karen   No, they're not **her / hers**. See the keychain? It says "Andy."

Matt   I lost **my / mine** glasses, too!

Karen   Wait a minute. Is this jacket **your / yours**?

Matt   Yes, thanks! You're amazing. Now, do you think you can find **my / mine** glasses?

3 About you

Grammar and vocabulary | Are these sentences true or false for you? Write *T* (true) or *F* (false). Then correct the false sentences.

1. I can never find anything in my closet. ___F___

   I can usually find things in my closet, but I can't find things in my drawers.

2. All my pens are in a jar on my desk. _____

   _____

3. I put things like my ID card and passport in a drawer in my dresser. _____

   _____

4. There's a box under my bed with photos and letters in it. _____

   _____

5. I put all my old magazines and books in the closet. _____

   _____

6. I keep stuff like shampoo, brushes, and my hair dryer in a drawer. _____

   _____

7. I keep all my shoes in the closet. _____

   _____

Things at home

1 Rooms and things

Vocabulary | **A** There are 20 home items in the puzzle. Find the other 18. Look in these directions (→↓).

Q	A	R	M	C	H	A	I	R	Q	W	T	B	A
R	U	B	H	T	K	V	P	G	H	M	L	A	J
L	E	C	A	R	P	E	T	U	K	I	Y	T	K
E	K	F	S	S	A	L	Q	W	E	R	R	H	C
S	D	I	S	H	W	A	S	H	E	R	F	T	C
E	R	S	T	O	V	M	O	A	P	O	B	U	U
R	E	C	O	W	T	P	F	E	M	R	G	B	R
C	S	O	V	E	N	N	A	F	A	U	C	E	T
A	S	A	E	R	B	U	K	R	W	C	L	O	A
B	E	M	I	C	R	O	W	A	V	E	Z	A	I
I	R	Q	U	X	L	S	I	N	K	I	K	Z	N
N	M	N	I	G	H	T	S	T	A	N	D	E	S
E	S	E	C	U	S	H	I	O	N	S	R	X	Z
T	O	I	L	E	T	R	E	S	Y	L	V	A	D
S	F	A	C	O	F	F	E	E	T	A	B	L	E

B Read the clues and write the rooms in the center of the webs. Then complete the webs with words from part A. Some words can be used more than once.

1. I sleep in this room.

2. I cook and sometimes eat in this room.

3. I wash my face and brush my teeth in this room.

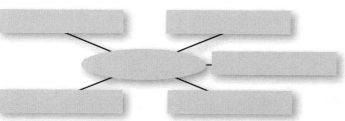

4. In this room, I listen to music, watch TV, and relax.

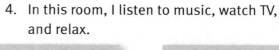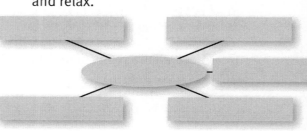

2 I like that one.

Grammar | Look at the pictures. Complete Ana's questions with *one* or *ones*. Bob has different tastes.
Write his answers using two adjectives and a prepositional phrase.

1. **Ana** I like the Thai sofa. Which ___*one*___ do you like?
    Bob *Oh, I like the big Italian one on the right.*

2. **Ana** I like the white dresser. Which _____ do you like?
    Bob _____

3. **Ana** I like the square mirrors. Which _____ do you like?
    Bob _____

4. **Ana** I love the big clock. Which _____ do you like?
    Bob _____

3 Susan's living room

Grammar and vocabulary | Unscramble the sentences about Susan's living room.

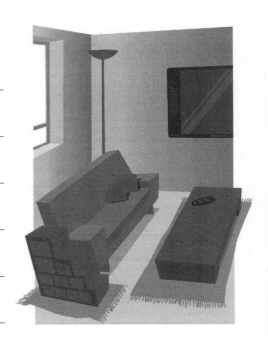

1. small / living room / There's / a / sofa / in / her
    There's a small sofa in her living room.

2. has / square / some / cool / cushions / She / on the sofa
    _____

3. in front of / There's / a / the / coffee table / sofa / long / dark
    _____

4. a / TV / She / big / on the wall / has / black
    _____

5. lamp / a / There's / tall / in the corner / Italian
    _____

6. are / on the floor / some / cotton / nice / rugs / There
    _____

1 Asking politely

Conversation
strategies | Complete the questions with *Would you mind* or *Do you mind if*.

1. A *Do you mind if* I borrow your dictionary?
   B No, not at all. Go ahead.

2. A _____ answering the phone for me?
   B Oh, no. No problem.

3. A _____ closing that door?
   B No, not at all.

4. A _____ I take off my shoes?
   B No. Go right ahead.

5. A _____ I use your laptop for a minute?
   B No problem.

6. A _____ handing me the potato salad?
   B Oh, no. Not at all. Here you go.

7. A _____ playing that song again?
   B I'd be happy to.

8. A _____ I eat the last piece of apple pie?
   B Not at all. Go ahead.

9. A _____ I turn on the news for a minute?
   B No, not at all.

10. A _____ turning down the music a little?
    B No problem.

2 No problem.

Circle the correct responses to complete the conversation.

Mother Rudy, do you have a minute?

Rudy (Sure.)/ **No, not at all.** What's the matter?

Mother Well, your grandparents are on their way, and the house is a mess. Could you please clean your room before they get here?

Rudy **No, go right ahead. / OK.** I can do it now.

Mother Oh, and would you mind taking your weight-training things out of the living room?

Rudy **Sure. No problem. / Yes.** But do you mind if I do it after I clean my room?

Mother **No, of course not. / Sure, I'd be happy to.** Actually, I should probably call your grandparents to make sure they're not lost. Where's my phone?

Rudy Um, I don't know.

Mother Hmm. Can I borrow your phone for a minute?

Rudy **No. Go right ahead. / Sure, go ahead.**

Mother Where is it?

Rudy Uh . . . I don't know. I think it's here somewhere. . . .

3 Requests, requests

Agree to these requests from a visitor to your home. Then add a question.

1. A I feel sleepy. Would you mind making some coffee?
   B *No, not at all. How you do like it?*

2. A Do you mind if we watch the soccer game tonight?
   B _____

3. A I feel hot. Could I get a glass of water?
   B _____

4. A Can I borrow your phone? I need to call my sister.
   B _____

5. A Sorry, I can't hear you. Would you mind turning down the music a little?
   B _____

6. A Can we listen to some music?
   B _____

7. A I feel a little hungry. Do you mind if I take an apple?
   B _____

8. A Could I borrow a sweater? I feel a little cold.
   B _____

1 Cat habitat

Reading | **A** What do you think these words mean?

| cat boat | cat lady | houseboat | stray cat |

B Read the article and check the meanings of the words in part A.

All aboard, furry neighbors!

Have you ever lived next door to a boat? How about a boat full of cats?

Amsterdam, the largest city in the Netherlands, is full of canals. There are many different kinds of boats on the canals. Some of them carry people and goods, some have shops or restaurants on them, while others are houseboats – boats that people live on. But not only people live on these houseboats. Cats do too, at least on two of them.

It all began in 1966 with a stray cat, her kittens, and a kind woman named Henriette van Weelde. One rainy night, Henriette heard a cat crying outside her house. She opened the door and saw a wet mother cat trying to protect her kittens from the rain. Henriette felt sorry for the poor animals, so she let them live with her. Soon another stray cat joined them, and then more. Henriette quickly became known as the "cat lady."

Before long, the cats filled Henriette's house. Then they filled her garden. And the cats kept coming. What could she do with them all? She saw the answer to her problem floating on the canal – a houseboat. People could live on houseboats, so why couldn't cats? In 1968, Henriette bought her first "cat boat."

Soon, even more stray cats moved in, and then came people who wanted to help – the first volunteers. But after just three years, the houseboat was full of cats. So Henriette bought another boat! More people were visiting, not just to bring cats in, but also to adopt a pet or just to look. After all, a houseboat for cats is not a common sight!

Today, Henriette's two cat boats are still in the same place on the canal. And the Cat Boat Foundation that Henriette started years ago is not only an official Dutch charity but also an international tourist attraction!

C Read these questions. Find the answers in the article.

1. What do the boats on Amsterdam's canals do? _They carry people and goods. Some of them are shops and restaurants. People live on them, too._

2. Why did Henriette van Weelde take in the first stray cat? _____

3. What did Henriette do when her house and garden filled with cats? _____

4. Who helped Henriette take care of the cats? _____

5. What are two reasons people visit Henriette's cat boats? _____

2 A typical Sunday

Writing **A Read the statements. Choose the correct words to complete the sentences.**

1. ___First___, Danny wakes up around noon on Sunday. (first / as soon as)
2. He sleeps for 30 or so minutes more _____ he gets out of bed. (before / after)
3. _____, he takes a quick shower, gets dressed, and goes downstairs. (then / while)
4. _____, he goes into the kitchen and makes a huge breakfast. (when / next)
5. _____ he's eating breakfast, he reads the sports section of the paper. (during / while)
6. He checks his email _____ he finishes his breakfast. (when / next)
7. He watches football on TV _____ he's off the computer. (as soon as / then)
8. He usually falls asleep once or twice _____ the game. (during / while)
9. _____ the game is over, Danny goes upstairs and takes a long nap. (then / after)

B Write true sentences about your Sunday afternoons. Use *first, next, then, before, after, during, as soon as, while,* and *when*.

First, I

Unit 8 Progress chart

What can you do? Mark the boxes. ☑ = I can . . . ? = I need to review how to . . .	To review, go back to these pages in the Student's Book.
Grammar	
ask questions with *Whose.*	76 and 77
use possessive pronouns.	76 and 77
order adjectives before nouns, and before the pronouns *one* and *ones.*	79
use location expressions after nouns and pronouns.	79
Vocabulary	
name at least 6 places to keep things in my home.	75
name at least 15 home items for different rooms.	78
Conversation strategies	
request permission politely to do things with *Do you mind if . . . ?*	80 and 81
make requests politely with *Would you mind . . . ?*	80 and 81
agree to requests in different ways.	81
Writing	
order events using sequencing words.	83

65

1 What were they doing?

Grammar | Circle the correct verb forms in these stories.

1. A friend and I **ran** / (**were running**) in the park, and this guy **rode** / **was riding** behind us. We didn't hear him because we **listened** / **were listening** to music. Anyway, we **decided** / **were deciding** to stop because I was tired, and the guy **ran** / **was running** right into me. And then he just **rode** / **was riding** away!

2. An embarrassing thing **happened** / **was happening** when I **studied** / **was studying** singing at the university. At my first concert, I was on the stage and I **saw** / **was seeing** a concert hall full of people. I **got** / **was getting** so scared that I completely **forgot** / **was forgetting** the words to my song. So I just **stood** / **was standing** on the stage, and I **said** / **was saying**, "Thank you." After that, I **walked** / **was walking** off and **went** / **was going** home.

2 Interruptions

Grammar | Complete the stories with the verbs given. Use one simple past verb and one past continuous verb in each sentence.

1. I _was telling_ (tell) my friends a funny story about my brother, and he _____ (walk) in.

2. I _____ (do) my laundry, and I _____ (hear) a noise. My phone was in the washing machine.

3. My dad _____ (delete) my music files when he _____ (try) to fix my computer.

4. A friend and I _____ (have) lunch when our server _____ (spill) coffee all over us.

5. My mom and dad _____ (saw) one of their neighbors on the same plane when they _____ (fly) to Beijing.

6. My teacher _____ (talk) on her cell phone, and she _____ (run) right into me in the hallway.

3 Telling anecdotes

Grammar and vocabulary | Look at the pictures. Write sentences using the past continuous and the simple past.

1. *A guy was having his lunch in the park. He was reading.*
   _____
   _____
   _____

2. _____
   _____
   _____
   _____

4 About you

Grammar | Think about your week. Complete the sentences with true information.

1. When I was eating dinner a couple of nights ago, *I spilled spaghetti sauce on my favorite T-shirt* .
2. My friend called me when I _____ last weekend.
3. I was doing my homework one night when _____.
4. Last week, I was going to class, and I _____.
5. Last weekend, I _____
   when I _____.
6. Yesterday, I was talking to a friend and _____.

1 Parts of the body

Reading **A** Look at the pictures and complete the puzzle.

Down

Across

B Circle the correct words and complete the sentences.

1. I can't move. I hurt my ___back___ .
   a. thumb   b. back   c. arm

2. It's hard to walk. I broke my _____ .
   a. nose   b. leg   c. shoulder

3. I got a bruise on my _____ . It hurts to smile.
   a. finger   b. toe   c. face

4. I sprained my _____ , so it's hard to write.
   a. wrist   b. ankle   c. chest

5. It hurts to wear high heels. I broke my _____ .
   a. finger   b. shoulder   c. toe

6. I got a black _____ . I can't see clearly.
   a. eye   b. head   c. neck

7. I can't bend my arm. I hurt my _____ .
   a. elbow   b. hip   c. knee

8. It's hard to wash dishes. I cut my _____ .
   a. knee   b. foot   c. hand

9. I hurt my _____ . I can't turn my head.
   a. thumb   b. neck   c. wrist

10. I broke my _____ . It's hard to breathe.
    a. nose   b. hip   c. eye

2 How did you hurt yourself?

Grammar | **Complete the conversations. Use reflexive pronouns.**

1. A How did your sister hurt her hand?

   B Oh, she burned _____ when she was making tea.

2. A Are you OK? Did you hurt your ankle?

   B Yeah. I fell when I was jogging. I didn't hurt _____ badly.

3. A What happened to your friends?

   B Oh, they hurt _____ when they were moving to a new apartment.

4. A How did your father cut _____?

   B He was chopping vegetables for dinner.

3 A wonderful day

Grammar | **Complete the conversation. Write the questions using the past continuous.**

Mom   Hi, honey. How was your day?

Alicia   Well, I hurt myself. I kicked a ball, and it hit me on the head.

Mom   Oh, no! *What were you doing?*
              (What)

Alicia   Well, I was playing soccer with some friends. I was looking in the other direction.

Mom   _____
              (Why)

Alicia   Well, I was looking at a guy. I guess I wasn't paying attention.

Mom   _____
              (Who)

Alicia   This really cute guy named Jason.

Mom   _____
              (Was)

Alicia   No, he wasn't playing with us. He was just standing there.

Mom   _____
              (Where)

Alicia   In front of the field. He was talking on the phone. Anyway, I kicked the ball, the ball hit Jason, and then it hit me.

Mom   That's terrible!

Alicia   Not really. Now I have a date with him on Saturday!

1 I bet you felt bad!

Conversation strategies | **Number the sentences in the conversation in the correct order.**

1. _____ Australia? That sounds like a fun trip.

   __1__ You won't believe what I did last week. I was riding my bike with a friend in City Park.

   _____ Yeah. But anyway, I wasn't paying attention and ran right into a woman in front of me.

   _____ Yeah, it is. Anyway, my friend and I were talking about going to Australia.

   _____ Oh, that's a beautiful park.

   _____ Oh, no! I bet she wasn't too happy!

2. _____ Yeah. So I jumped out of bed, got dressed, and ran all the way to school.

   _____ You're kidding! That late?

   _____ I bet no one even noticed.

   _____ Yeah, I was. And when I got to class, I saw that I was wearing two different sneakers. One blue and one black! But anyway, everyone was studying for a test. So I just sat at the back.

   _____ Guess what I did? I woke up late this morning, and it was after 10:30.

   _____ The whole way? I bet you were exhausted!

3. _____ I know. The horse fell right on top of her, and she couldn't get up. But my father was there.

   _____ Yeah, it was. My dad took her to the hospital, and she's OK now.

   _____ Do you remember my cousin, Courtney? Well, one day last summer she was out riding when her horse fell.

   _____ That was lucky!

   _____ Oh, my gosh! That's awful.

   _____ Thank goodness.

2 I bet . . .

Conversation strategies | **Complete each conversation with an appropriate response using *I bet*.**

1. A I was at the mall the other day, and I walked right into a glass door! I was so embarrassed.
   B *I bet no one even noticed.*

2. A My sister wasn't paying attention when she left home for work this morning, and she locked herself out of her apartment.

   B _____

3. A My little sister borrowed my new laptop last night, and she dropped it! So now it's not working.

   B _____

4. A I went to a concert with some friends last weekend, but I was so bored that I fell asleep!

   B _____

5. A I went to the car wash yesterday and forgot to close the car window. I got so wet!

   B _____

6. A Guess what? I just won a trip to Miami in a radio contest!

   B _____

3 And then what happened?

Conversation strategies | **Finish these anecdotes. Then write an appropriate response.**

1. A I was walking to work one morning, and I thought I saw my old friend from middle school
   across the street. *So I ran after him and called his name.*
   Anyway, he turned around and it wasn't my friend at all.
   B *Oh, no! I bet you were embarrassed.*

2. A I was taking a taxi once, and I was in a hurry. I wanted to pay with my credit
   card but _____

   _____

   _____

   B _____

3. A Last year, none of my friends called to wish me Happy Birthday. I thought, "Maybe they
   just forgot." Well, when I got home, I opened the door and _____

   _____

   B _____

4. A My brother was driving my dad's car in a bad storm one night and _____

   _____

   _____

   B _____

Acts of kindness

Reading | **A Read the article. Find the answers to these questions.**

1. Who is Nelson Hunter?
2. Who found Andrea's wallet?

3. How did Abby get home?
4. What did John get?

Around Town *by Nelson Hunter*

A few weeks ago, I was walking to my car in the parking lot, when someone came up to me and said he enjoyed reading my weekly column. "But," he said, "you always write about everyone's bad experiences. Why don't you ask people to talk about their good experiences, too?"

So I asked readers to write in and tell me about all the good things that happened to them recently. I got hundreds of replies. Here are three of them:

When I was shopping at the mall last week, I lost my wallet with all my money and credit cards in it. I spent a long time looking for it with no luck. I was really upset because it had my spare house key and my address in it, too. Anyway, later that day after I got home, my doorbell rang. It was a young man, and he had my wallet. Apparently, he saw it on the ground when he was walking into the mall. He drove all the way to my house to give it to me! I couldn't believe it! I was so lucky!

– Andrea Keane

I was coming home from a party really late at night, and I missed the last train home. I didn't have enough money for a cab, and I didn't want to walk home in the dark. I was standing outside the train station, and I guess I looked worried because a woman came up and asked me if I needed any help. She offered to share a cab with me and to pay for it! She said she didn't like being by herself at night, either. I was so grateful.

– Abby Walters

After class each week, I often go to the local donut shop and get some coffee before I go home. When I was leaving the store last week, the owner gave me a bag of donuts from the day before to take home for free. She said I was a good customer, and she didn't want to throw them out. When I got home, I shared them with my roommates!

– John Jones

So, thank you for all the letters. For next week, I want to hear about any funny stories you have. What funny things happened to you recently?

B Read the article again. Write *T* (true) or *F* (false) for each sentence. Then correct the false sentences.

1. Nelson Hunter usually writes about bad things that happen to people. __*T*__
2. Andrea was worried because if someone found her wallet, they could get into her house. _____
3. A young man found Andrea's wallet when he was leaving the mall. _____
4. Abby Walters had to pay for a cab home when she missed her train. _____
5. John ate the bag of donuts by himself. _____

Things happen **UNIT 9**

2 Two unusual events

Writing | **A** Read about two unusual events. Complete the stories using *when* or *while*. Sometimes both are correct.

❶ Years ago, ___*when*___ my friend and I were in middle school, we decided to write our names on a one-dollar bill for fun. We spent the money and forgot about it. Then, one night about 20 years later, _____ I was waiting for a bus, I saw a dollar bill on the street. I picked it up, and my name was on it. It was the same bill we wrote on! _____ I think of it now, I'm amazed!

– Ken Leonard, Los Angeles

❷ I had a strange experience a couple of months ago. It happened one night _____ I was sleeping. It was probably about two in the morning _____ I woke up to loud music. _____ I looked around, I saw that the radio was on. I clearly remember turning it off _____ I went to bed.

– Lisa Lee, Hong Kong

B Write about an unusual event that happened to you or to someone you know.

A really unusual thing happened to

Unit 9 Progress chart

What can you do? Mark the boxes. ✓ = I can . . . ? = I need to review how to . . .	To review, go back to these pages in the Student's Book.
Grammar make past continuous statements.	86 and 87
ask past continuous questions.	89
use reflexive pronouns.	89
Vocabulary name at least 12 parts of the body.	88
name at least 6 injuries.	88 and 89
Conversation strategies react to and comment on a story.	90 and 91
respond with *I bet*.	91
Writing link ideas with *when* and *while*.	93

73

Communication

Lesson A — Keeping in touch

1 Bigger and better

Grammar **A** Complete the chart below with the comparative form of the adjectives in the box.

✓bad	cheap	easy	hard	noisy	quick
big	convenient	expensive	important	old	slow
boring	cool	fun	interesting	personal	small
busy	difficult	good	new	popular	useful

Adjective + -er / -ier		more / less + adjective		Irregular adjectives	
				worse	

B Complete the sentences with the comparative form of the adjectives.

1. Postcards are _____*slower*_____ (slow) than email.

2. Cell-phone service is _____ (expensive) than regular phone service.

3. Texting is often _____ (easy) than sending an email.

4. I think sending e-cards is _____ (convenient) than sending regular cards.

5. To me, black and white photos are _____ (nice) than color photos.

6. I think pop-up ads are _____ (bad) than spam.

7. It's _____ (important) to have a phone than to have a computer.

8. Tablets are _____ (good) than laptops when you're working on the bus.

C Complete the conversation with the comparative form of the adjectives. Add *than* where necessary. Some adjectives need *less*.

Dong-Un I love my new tablet. It's so much _*better than*_ (good) my old laptop.

Loni I know. And the new tablets are _____ (expensive), too. Some cost only $200. Actually, this one was much _____ (cheap) my laptop.

Dong-Un And they're _____ (convenient) laptops. They're _____ (fun), too. I like the touch screen. And they have a _____ (long) battery life, too.

Loni Right. I know laptops are _____ (popular) tablets these days, but I like my old laptop. It has a _____ (big) memory. And it's _____ (easy) to work on when I have to write long papers.

Dong-Un Yeah, but it sure is a lot _____ (heavy) a tablet!

2 It's quieter than the office.

Grammar | Complete the comments with the comparative form of the adjectives. Add *than* where necessary. Some adjectives need *less*.

1. My boss works on the bus. He says it's
   quieter than (quiet) the office. He thinks
   there's nothing _____ (bad) other
   people's cell phone conversations on the bus.

2. My friend doesn't like e-cards. She says
   they're _____ (personal) real cards.
   Actually, I think they're _____ (fun)
   because you can add music and stuff.

3. My dad isn't good with computers. My mom is
   much _____ (good) than he is, but
   she prefers to talk on the phone. She says it's
   _____ (easy) to talk and do other
   things at the same time.

4. My co-workers think video conferencing is
   _____ (convenient) business trips.
   It's also _____ (tiring) because you
   don't get jet lag.

3 I don't think so!

Grammar and vocabulary | Write a response to disagree with the statements.

1. A I think tablets are harder to use than smartphones.
   B _Really? I think tablets are easier to use than smartphones._

2. A Cameras take better photos than the cameras in cell phones.
   B _____

3. A I think it's more important to listen to the radio than watch TV.
   B _____

4. A It's easier to understand a voice-mail message in English than a written note.
   B _____

5. A It's worse to have no phone than to have no laptop.
   B _____

6. A I think text messages are more popular than phone calls.
   B _____

1 Phone situations

Vocabulary | **A** Choose the correct word to complete each phone expression.

1. call me __c__   a. number   b. off   c. back
2. have another _____   a. call   b. number   c. mistake
3. leave a _____   a. back   b. message   c. call
4. have the wrong _____ a. number   b. mistake   c. another
5. hold _____   a. on   b. in   c. call
6. get cut _____   a. back   b. on   c. off
7. break _____   a. back   b. up   c. on

B Use the phone expressions above to complete the sentences. Use the correct form of the verbs.

1. One of my friends called me at work, but I was in an important meeting and couldn't talk. I asked him to _call me back_ later.

2. I'm trying to call my sister, but I can't hear her. She's in the mountains, and the call keeps _____ .

3. I need to talk to my grandmother, but she's not home. I want her to return my call, so I should probably _____ .

4. My brother tried to call his office, but he accidentally called someone he didn't know. He _____ .

5. I have problems with my cell phone. Every time I walk into my bedroom, I hear a click and then I _____ .

6. I called my brother, but his wife said he was upstairs watching TV. She asked me to _____ while she called him to the phone.

7. My mom works at home, and she gets a lot of phone calls. Every time I call her, I have to hold on because she _____ .

2 How do they respond?

Grammar and vocabulary **Circle the best response for each phone expression.**

1. I can't hear you. You're breaking up.
   a. I have another call.
   b. Call me back later.

2. Please leave a message.
   a. Hi, Frank. This is Manny. Call me at home.
   b. Good-bye.

3. Can you hold on, please?
   a. Sure, no problem.
   b. I got cut off.

4. Oh, I'm sorry. I think I have the wrong number.
   a. One moment, please.
   b. No problem.

5. Good morning, Cambridge University Press.
   a. Would you like to leave a message?
   b. Could I speak to Sally Smith, please?

6. Did you get my message?
   a. Yeah, I think I did.
   b. No problem.

3 More than you!

Grammar **Complete the sentences with *more*, *less*, or *fewer*.**

1. Nancy Wow! Look at your inbox. It's full of junk mail. You get a lot ___*more*___ junk mail than I do.

   Bill I know. I guess I get a lot of emails, generally. Look – 50 today.

   Nancy Yeah. I get about three or four a day. You get a lot _____ emails than I do.

2. Julie My cell phone bill was really high this month. I really need to make _____ calls. Or talk _____ than I do now. Look – it was $65.

   Paula Actually, that's not bad. Mine was $95. My cell phone costs _____ than yours.

3. Dan You know, I only had four text messages last month. I'm getting _____ text messages than phone calls. I guess people prefer to call me these days.

   Eric Yeah? Actually, I like instant messaging _____ than talking.

4. Miki Are you still working? You spend _____ time online than anyone I know.

   Larry I know. I really should work _____ and spend _____ time with you and the kids.

5. Ben Oh, no! The Internet is down again! I need to change my Internet service provider to yours. You seem to have _____ problems with your provider than I do.

   Paul Maybe. I know my Internet connection goes down _____ than yours, but it costs a lot _____ than yours, too.

1 Exciting news

Conversation strategies

A Read the conversation. Then complete the chart below with expressions from the conversation.

Ellen Tommy? It's Ellen. You won't believe it!

Tommy Sorry, Ellen. Can you hold on a minute? I have to turn the music down. . . . OK, what were you saying?

Ellen Remember that job interview I had last week?

Tommy Sure, I do. Oh, just a second. My cell phone's ringing. . . . So, where were we?

Ellen My job interview last week. They called this morning and – oops! Excuse me just a minute. I spilled my tea. . . . What was I saying?

Tommy They called about the job. . . .

Ellen Yeah, right. I got the job! I start next month.

Tommy Next month? That's great! Oh, just a minute. I need to close the window . . . OK, so you were saying?

Ellen This is the exciting part! Can you wait just a second? I need to turn off the stove. . . . All right. Where was I?

Tommy The exciting part about your new job.

Ellen Right! They want me to work in their London office!

Tommy That's amazing! Congratulations, Ellen!

Interrupting a conversation	Restarting a conversation
1. *Can you hold on a minute?*	1. *OK, what were you saying?*
2.	2.
3.	3.
4.	4.
5.	5.

B Complete the conversations with the expressions from the chart above. Sometimes there is more than one correct answer.

1. **Nolan** Hi, Akemi! I have some good news.
   Akemi Oh, I'm sorry. _____ I have another call.
   Nolan Sure, go ahead.

2. **Abby** Kyle, it's Abby. I'm at the supermarket and . . .
   Kyle Just a second. I have to turn off the TV. _____
   Abby I was saying, I'm at the supermarket. Can you come pick me up?

3. **Muriel** Hey, it's me. I'm calling because I'm – oops! Hold on, I dropped my briefcase. . . . _____
   Brett You're calling because you're . . .
   Muriel Oh, yes, I'm working late. I'll be home around nine tonight.

2 I just need to . . .

Conversation
strategies **Add *just* to the sentences to make them softer.**

1. I need to ask you a few questions.   *I just need to ask you a few questions.*

2. Sure. Can you wait a minute?   _____

3. I have to answer the door.   _____

4. Could you hold on a second?   _____

5. I need to turn off the faucet.   _____

6. Sorry. I need to take another call.   _____

7. I'm calling to find out about your test.   _____

8. I have to tell you one thing.   _____

3 Hold on a second

Conversation
strategies **Imagine a friend calls. Follow the instructions and complete the conversation.
Use *just* where possible.**

You   Hello?

Friend   Hi, it's me! Hey, I was just calling to tell you, this weekend there's . . .

You   *Oh, can you hold on a second? I just want to turn down the music.*
    OK. Sorry. So, what were you saying?
    (Interrupt to turn down the music. Restart the conversation.)

Friend   I was just calling to tell you about my party this weekend.

You   Great. So, what's the special . . . _____

    _____
    (Interrupt because you have another call. Ask your friend to call you back.)

Friend   Hey.

You   Hi. Sorry about that. So, _____
    (Restart the conversation.)

Friend   My party – this weekend.

You   Right. _____
    (Interrupt to answer the door.)

    Sorry. So, are you having a birthday party?

Friend   No. It's just for fun. I'm going to invite . . .

You   _____

    Oh, that's better.

    _____
    (Interrupt because the call is breaking up. Restart the conversation.)

Friend   Oh, I was saying, I'm going to invite everyone from class. So . . .

You   _____
    (Interrupt because your battery is running out. Say you can call back.)

Friend   Hi, again.

You   _____
    (Restart the conversation.)

Friend   I was saying that everybody in the class is invited. So, can you come?

You   Oh, yeah, I'd love to. Thanks.

1 Drawing crowds

Reading **A** Read the definitions of *crowd* and *outsourcing*, and guess the meaning of *crowdsourcing*.
Then read the article to check your guess.

Crowd: a large group of people   *Outsourcing*: getting outside workers to do jobs for a business

Crowdsourcing is:

- A website about a particular topic.
- A large group of volunteers completing a task together.
- A free Internet encyclopedia.

CROWDSOURCING

What can bring together a big crowd? A football game or a rock concert can fill a stadium with people. But big crowds also bring big problems to solve, like security or cleaning up after the event. The people in charge often outsource these jobs to security and cleaning companies.

Can you imagine a rock band asking the audience to volunteer to clean up before they leave? That is the basic idea of crowdsourcing – using a large group of volunteers to work together on a project. The word *crowdsourcing* is a combination of the words *crowd* and *outsource*.

Crowdsourced websites, such as wikis and social networking sites, are some of the most successful Internet organizations. Wikis offer millions of people free online information on a variety of topics. Almost 100,000 volunteers from around the world write and edit the topics in many different languages. Social networking websites also use crowdsourcing. They connect users to stories, ideas, opinions, and news, and they give people instant access to information from many sources. This information is often not available in traditional media such as news websites or TV news.

Wikis are some of the most visited websites in the world. However, many critics disapprove of their structure. They argue volunteers don't have the expertise to write about some topics. They also claim a lot of wiki articles are poorly written. Another issue is that wikis and social networking websites are only as useful as their network size. Some wikis and social networking websites fail because they do not have a big enough crowd to provide much interesting information.

Crowdsourcing has some problems. On the other hand, it is a useful way to complete large projects. It shows that when lots of individuals contribute a small amount of time and energy, it quickly adds up to a significant result.

B Read the article again. Write *T* (true) or *F* (false) for each sentence. Then correct the false sentences.

1. *Outsourcing* means using somebody inside a business to do work. _____
2. Wikis don't pay people to write articles for them. _____
3. Almost 10,000 people around the world write articles for wikis. _____
4. Social networking websites need large crowds to succeed. _____

2 Pros and cons

Writing | **A** Match each section of a short article to the correct sentence.

Section	Summary
1. Introduction to the topic of crowdsourcing <u>_b_</u>	a. Crowdsourcing has pros and cons, but it also has significant results.
2. Advantages of crowdsourcing _____	✓b. *Crowdsourcing* means using a large group of volunteers to complete a project.
3. Disadvantages of crowdsourcing _____	c. Crowdsourced websites offer millions of people free information, news, and opinions often not available in traditional media.
4. Conclusion _____	d. However, information is not always correct on crowdsourced websites, and their crowds are not always large enough to be useful.

B Write a short article on a popular crowdsourcing website. Include an introduction, the advantages, the disadvantages, and a conclusion.

_____ _____ *is very popular these days*

Unit 10 Progress chart

What can you do? Mark the boxes. ✓ = I can . . . ? = I need to review how to . . .	To review, go back to these pages in the Student's Book.
Grammar	☐ make comparisons with adjectives. ☐ use *more*, *less*, and *fewer* with nouns and verbs.	98 and 99 101
Vocabulary	☐ name at least 6 kinds of electronic communication. ☐ use at least 5 different phone expressions.	97 and 98 100 and 101
Conversation strategies	☐ interrupt and restart conversations on the phone. ☐ use *just* to soften things I say.	102 and 103 103
Writing	☐ write an article including the advantages and disadvantages of a topic, and a conclusion with my views.	105

Lesson A / Family traits

1 What's wrong?

Grammar
and
vocabulary | Look at the pictures. Correct the three mistakes in each description.

1. Teresa is old. She's a little heavy. She's got long
   blond hair. She looks a lot like Megan. She's wearing
   a black sweater.

   Teresa isn't old. She's young.

   _____

   _____

2. Megan is young. She's slim with long straight hair. She
   looks a lot like Teresa. She's wearing a white sweater.

   _____

   _____

   _____

2 Do you look alike?

Grammar | Complete the conversation with the missing questions. Sometimes there is
more than one correct answer.

Kari	Did you meet my brother Bob at the party last night? He's home for spring break.
David	I'm not sure. Does he look like you? I mean, *do you look alike?* _____
Kari	No, we look totally different.
David	Huh. So, _____?
Kari	He's six four. He's a lot taller than me.
David	Wow. And _____?
Kari	No, he doesn't. It's very curly. But it's blond like mine.
David	Then it's not the guy I'm thinking of. _____?
Kari	He's 21. So he's younger than me.
David	Oh, OK. _____? Are they green?
Kari	Yes, he's got green eyes. Oh, look. He's here now.
David	Oh, him! So, _____?
Kari	Actually, he takes after my mom. And I look like my dad.

3 A family portrait

Grammar and vocabulary **Look at the picture and answer the questions.**

1. Who does Karen take after, Sharon or Dick? *She takes after Sharon.*

2. Who's got dark hair? _____

3. Do all the women have straight hair? _____

4. Do Kevin and Joey look alike? _____

5. Who do Kevin and Joey take after? _____

4 About you

Grammar and vocabulary **Answer the questions with true information.**

1. How tall are you? Are you taller or shorter than your parents?
   I'm taller than my mother, but I'm shorter than my father.

2. Do you take after your father or your mother? How?

   _____

3. Who does your father take after, his mother or his father? How?

   _____

4. How many people have dark hair in your family? Does anyone have curly hair?

   _____

5. What color eyes do people in your family have?

   _____

1 What is it?

Vocabulary | **A Read the clues and write the features.**

1. They can make a person's teeth straight. _braces_
2. It grows on a man's chin. _____
3. They are tiny braids close to a person's head. _____
4. People wear them to see better. _____
5. They have tiny holes for wearing earrings. _____
6. People who do weight training usually get this way. _____
7. They are little brown spots on a person's face or body. _____
8. It grows under a man's nose. _____
9. This is what we call men with no hair. _____
10. Some women paint them to make their hands look nice. _____
11. People with long hair often wear it in one of these to keep their hair out of the way. _____
12. This is your hairstyle if your hair is short and stands up. _____

B Answer the questions with your own ideas and information.

1. Do you think men should have pierced ears? _No, I don't. I don't think men should wear jewelry._
   or _I think it's OK. Men wear rings and bracelets, so it's OK if they wear earrings, too._

2. Do you know anyone with freckles? _____
   _____

3. Did you ever wear braces on your teeth? _____
   _____

4. Which is better, being muscular or being thin? Why? _____
   _____

5. How many people in the class wear their hair in a ponytail? Does anyone wear braids or cornrows?
   _____
   _____

6. Do you know anyone with a shaved head, a beard, or a mustache? _____
   _____

7. Do any of your friends have spiked hair? Are any of them bald? _____
   _____

2 Which one?

Grammar and vocabulary | Look at the picture. Write a sentence about each student using the word given and one other descriptive phrase as in the example.

1. A Which one is Lisa? (check her grades)
   B _Lisa is the one in the black jeans checking her grades._

2. A Which one is Julio? (stand at the back)
   B _____

3. A Which one is Mei-ling? (listen to music)
   B _____

4. A Who is Luigi? (write an essay)
   B _____

5. A What about Ivy, which one is she? (sit at the front)
   B _____

6. A So which guy is Kareem? (wear a striped T-shirt)
   B _____

7. A Which one is Anna? (talk to Kareem)
   B _____

8. A Is Kazu here? Who is he? (read a book)
   B _____

What's his name?

1 I can't remember

Conversation
strategies | **Complete the conversations with the questions in the box.**

> What's his / her name?
> What do you call it / them?
> What do you call that thing / those things?

1. **Katherine** Hey, Yong-joon, you're a big soccer fan. We're trying to remember the name of that famous Brazilian player.
    What's his name?

    Yong-joon Do you mean Marcelo?

    Katherine I don't know. He's got short hair, and it sticks up on top. _____

    Yong-joon Spiked hair? Then it's not Marcelo. Maybe you're thinking of Neymar.

    Katherine Hmm. And then we're trying to remember the name of the guy with long hair, you know he wears it in those long twisted . . . _____

    Yong-joon Oh, you mean dreadlocks. You're thinking of Ronaldinho.

    Katherine Yes, that's one of the players. So who's the other one?

    Yong-joon I don't know. But you know, I think Ronaldinho looks different now. He often wears one of those wool hats . . .
    Oh, _____

    Katherine Oh, a beanie. Really?

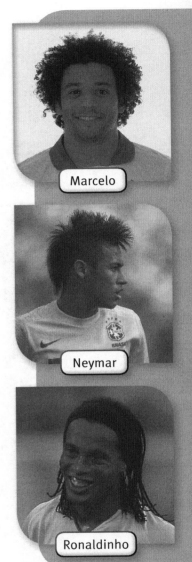

Marcelo

Neymar

Ronaldinho

2. **Brittany** Guess who we just saw at the airport! That singer, she has a really fabulous voice. _____?

    Ashley Um, Beyoncé?

    Brittany No. Not Beyoncé. She plays the piano and writes her own songs.

    Ashley Oh, I know who you mean. Years ago, she wore her hair in those little braids. _____?

    Brittany You mean cornrows. And she sang at that big game.
    Oh, _____? The um, the Superbowl.

    Ashley Oh, you mean Alicia Keys?

    Brittany Yeah. That's it. Well, we saw her at the airport.

Alicia Keys

2 Oh, you mean . . .

Conversation strategies | Who are they talking about? Respond using *You mean* . . . or *Do you mean* . . . ?
Then match the pictures.

a

Michelle Wie

1. A Who's that Mexican actress – the one who played
Frida Kahlo in that movie?

   B *Oh, you mean Salma Hayek.*   *d*

2. A I really like those tennis players . . . what are their names?
They're sisters with the cool tennis outfits.

   B _____   ____

b

Black Eyed Peas

c

Johnny Depp

3. A Do you want to go see that hip-hop band? You know,
the one with the female singer?

   B _____   ____

4. A My friend just loves that golfer. You know – the
really tall woman.

   B _____   ____

d

Salma Hayek

e

Venus and Serena Williams

5. A I really like that actor – what's his name? – he's in
Pirates of the Caribbean.

   B _____   ____

3 Describe it.

Look at the pictures. Complete the descriptions without using the actual word(s).
Then respond with *You mean* . . . or *Do you mean* . . . ?

1. A My sister loves to wear *those fancy women's shoes.*
They make women look really tall.

   B *Do you mean high heels?*

2. A My brother's hair _____

   _____

   B _____

3. A I just bought some of those pants with _____

   _____

   B _____

4. A My father has _____

   _____

   B _____

1 Hair trends

Reading | **A** Look at the pictures. Then read the article. Match each picture with a decade.

70s

Hairstyles through the decades...

Do you know how people wore their hair 10, 20, or 30 years ago? Look back at some of the popular hairstyles of the last few decades. There are some styles that come back again and again.

The 1950s were the beginning of the "rock 'n' roll" era. In the early '50s, men had short hair, but singer Elvis Presley changed all that when he combed his long hair into a "pompadour" and "duck tail." The ponytail was a popular hairstyle for young women.

The '60s was the decade of the Beatles, who caused a sensation when they grew their hair long – to their ears! In the late '60s and the early '70s, the "hippie look" was in style. Men and women grew their hair very long, and a lot of men had beards. The "Afro" was a popular hairstyle for African-Americans and anyone with curly hair or "perms."

Punk rockers shocked everyone with their multicolored, spiky hair in the '70s. Then in the late '70s and '80s, soap opera stars made "big hair" popular – women wore their hair very long, curly, and full.

The "new romantic" women of the '80s wore hairstyles from the 19th century – long curly hair and French braids. For many men, the "mullet" cut (short on top and long in the back) was the hairstyle to have.

In the '90s, dyed hair became stylish. Both men and women started changing the color of their hair or adding highlights. Some men began to bleach their hair blond.

In the 2000s, many women changed to a more "natural" look with long hair, similar to the 1970 hippie look. Some men had designs shaved into their hair; others had a textured or layered look.

So, what's going to be next? Look around you. Do you see any styles that are really "new"?

B Read the article again. Write *T* (true) or *F* (false) for each sentence. Then correct the false sentences.

1. Before Elvis Presley, guys wore their hair in a pompadour. __*F*__

2. In the '60s, the Beatles had very short hair. _____

3. In the '70s, curly hair and long hair were fashionable. _____

4. In the '90s, more people started to change the color of their hair. _____

5. In the 2000s, women started using more hair products than ever before. _____

6. Musicians and singers started some of the fashions in the last 50 years. _____

2 What's "in"?

Writing **A Read the article. Replace each underlined adjective and expression with a similar one in the box. Sometimes there is more than one correct answer.**

fashionable	"in"	in style	"out"	out of style	popular	the "in" thing	✓trendy

Plan your new look!

You're ready to buy new clothes. But wait! Look in your own closet first. Find colors that are "in" *trendy* this season, and see if they match with clothes you already have. Look at the colorful clothes people are wearing. Black will always be <u>fashionable</u>, but it's no longer the only choice. Add some tops in strong colors, since they are <u>the "in" thing</u> this year.

Casual dress is slowly going <u>out of style</u>. For example, sportswear is not very <u>popular</u> these days. Your best bet is to buy classics that are going to be <u>in style</u> for a longer time. As for jeans, look for the <u>trendy</u> styles arriving in stores soon. Skinny jeans will soon be "<u>out</u>," so think carefully before buying.

Remember, you often need to try on a lot of different styles to get a look that is right for you. Don't forget to have fun!

B Write a short article about new fashion trends using the expressions in the box above.

Unit 11 Progress chart

What can you do? Mark the boxes. ☑ = I can . . . ? = I need to review how to . . .	To review, go back to these pages in the Student's Book.
Grammar ☐ use *have* and *have got* to describe people.	108 and 109
☐ use phrases with verb + *-ing* and prepositions to identify people.	111
Vocabulary ☐ name at least 14 expressions and adjectives to describe people.	110 and 111
Conversation strategies ☐ show that I'm trying to remember a word.	112 and 113
☐ use *You mean* . . . to help someone remember something.	113
Writing ☐ use expressions to describe trends.	115

1 Things that go together

Vocabulary | Complete these sentences with the expressions in the box.

ask for a promotion	finish this course	get a master's degree	study abroad
become a millionaire	✓ have a baby	retire	travel around

1. My brother and his wife are going to __*have a baby*__ in September – I think they'll name her Nina.
2. My uncle might _____ . He has his own business, and it's doing really well.
3. I think I'm ready for more responsibility at work. Maybe I'll _____ .
4. My cousin already has a degree in business, and he's going to _____ in economics this fall.
5. First, I want to _____ , and then I might take a harder class.
6. It won't be easy for my mom to _____ after working for 40 years.
7. My friends think it will be difficult to _____ because all the classes will be in English.
8. My cousins invited me to _____ Australia next summer, but I think it's going to be too expensive.

2 We might move!

Grammar | Circle the correct verbs to complete the sentences.

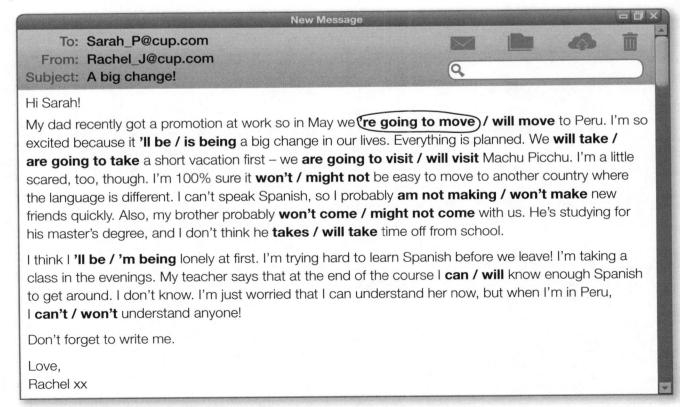

New Message

To: Sarah_P@cup.com
From: Rachel_J@cup.com
Subject: A big change!

Hi Sarah!

My dad recently got a promotion at work so in May we **'re going to move** / **will move** to Peru. I'm so excited because it **'ll be** / **is being** a big change in our lives. Everything is planned. We **will take** / **are going to take** a short vacation first – we **are going to visit** / **will visit** Machu Picchu. I'm a little scared, too, though. I'm 100% sure it **won't** / **might not** be easy to move to another country where the language is different. I can't speak Spanish, so I probably **am not making** / **won't make** new friends quickly. Also, my brother probably **won't come** / **might not come** with us. He's studying for his master's degree, and I don't think he **takes** / **will take** time off from school.

I think I **'ll be** / **'m being** lonely at first. I'm trying hard to learn Spanish before we leave! I'm taking a class in the evenings. My teacher says that at the end of the course I **can** / **will** know enough Spanish to get around. I don't know. I'm just worried that I can understand her now, but when I'm in Peru, I **can't** / **won't** understand anyone!

Don't forget to write me.

Love,
Rachel xx

3 Planning ahead

Grammar and vocabulary | Write two sentences about each picture. Use the words in parentheses and *be going to* or *will*. Sometimes there is more than one correct answer.

1. Linda has definite plans for next year. She has a place in college.

   She's going to study for a master's degree.
   (study for a master's degree)

   She isn't going to look for a job.
   (not look for a job)

2. Steve's not sure about his plans for the summer. He hopes to go away.

   _____
   (probably / go to Mexico)

   _____
   (not be able / go for long)

3. Betty and Clive made plans to retire this year.

   _____
   (retire in Arizona)

   _____
   (not retire / in New Mexico)

4. Sheena's taking acting classes. She wants to be a movie star.

   _____
   (be an actor)

   _____
   (maybe / be a star)

5. Simon is thinking about being a teacher. His favorite subject is math.

   _____
   (probably / teach math)

   _____
   (probably / not teach English)

6. Tim and Laura are excited about the summer because Laura is pregnant.

   _____
   (have a baby)

   _____
   (probably / not take a vacation)

1 What do they do?

Vocabulary | Write the names of the jobs under the pictures.

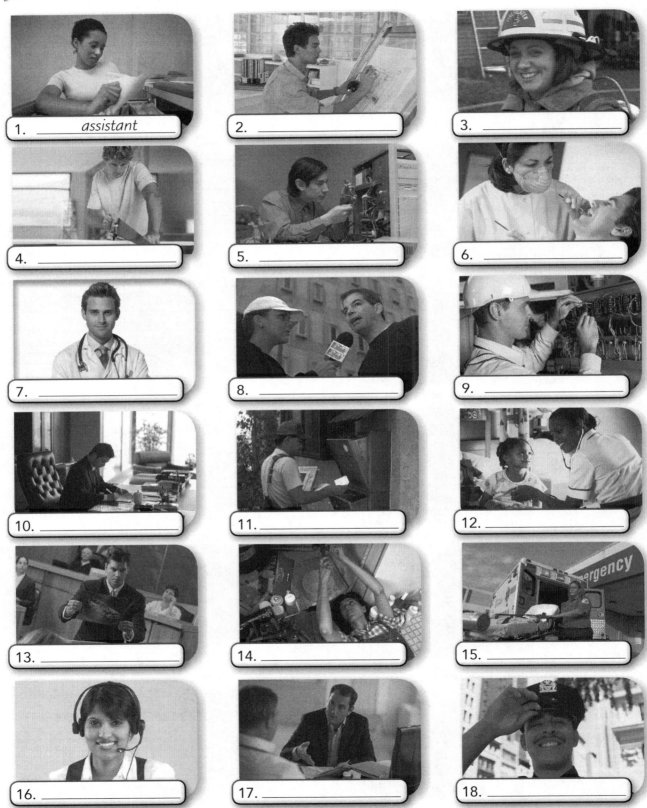

1. ___assistant___

2. _____

3. _____

4. _____

5. _____

6. _____

7. _____

8. _____

9. _____

10. _____

11. _____

12. _____

13. _____

14. _____

15. _____

16. _____

17. _____

18. _____

2 What are your plans?

Grammar | **Complete the conversations with the correct form of the verbs.**

1. Emily How's your job going?

   Beth OK. It _'ll be_ _____ better when I _____ my degree.

('ll be / 's) ('ll get / get)

   Emily Oh really? I guess after you _____ , you _____ more money.

('ll graduate / graduate) ('ll earn / earn)

   Beth That's right. And I _____ able to ask for a promotion, too if I _____

('ll be / 'm) ('ll get / get)
   really good grades.

   Emily Well, I'm sure all that hard work in night school is worth it.

   Beth I hope so. If I _____ pass the exams, I _____ and study full time.

(don't / won't) ('ll leave / leave)

2. Adam What are you going to do after we _____ college?

(finish / will finish)

   Neil I'm not sure. I _____ go to graduate school. How about you?

('ll / may)

   Adam Before I _____ any decisions, I think I _____ to my parents and ask

(make / 'll make) (talk / 'll talk)
   them for advice. If they can help me, I _____ my own business.

('ll start / start)

   Neil Sounds good. When your business _____ successful, will you give me a job

(is / will)
   after I _____ ?

(graduate / will graduate)

   Adam Sure. If you _____ nicely!

(ask / will ask)

3 About you

Grammar and vocabulary | **Complete the sentences with true information using *after*, *before*, *if*, or *when*.**

1. I'm sure my family will be really happy _when I get a master's degree_ .
2. I may study _____ .
3. I hope I'll be able to _____ .
4. I might not get _____ .
5. I guess I won't _____ .
6. I'll probably earn a lot of money _____ .
7. I'll be disappointed _____ .
8. One day I might, _____ .
9. I probably won't _____ .
10. I'll be really pleased _____ .

1 Promises, promises

Conversation
strategies
A Complete the conversations with the responses in the box.

> ✓ I'll make some salad.   If you want, I'll call and remind you.
> I won't forget.   I'll call you at 5:30, just in case.
> I'll wake up.   I'll lend you one.

1. Liam   Hey, Elaine! The class is having a picnic lunch on Saturday. Can you bring something?

   Elaine Sure. _I'll make some salad._

   Liam   Great! But don't forget the dressing like last time.

   Elaine _____ Well, I hope I won't.

   Liam   _____

   Elaine Yeah, that might be good. Thanks.

2. Jerry   Remember to set your alarm tonight. We're leaving at 6:00 a.m.

   Kevin   Uh, I lost my cell phone, but it's all right.

   Jerry   I don't know. You might oversleep.

   Kevin   Don't worry. _____

   Jerry   You know, I have two alarm clocks. _____

   Kevin   It's OK. Really. I always wake up early.

   Jerry   _____

   Kevin   OK, call me. Or maybe I should just stay at your place tonight. That way you won't worry!

B Make an offer or promise using the words given.

1. A Will you remember to call the plumber this afternoon?
   B Yes. _I won't forget._ (not forget)

2. A Oh, no! I forgot my cell phone. I have to call my brother for a ride home.
   B Don't worry. _____ you home. (drive)

3. A I'm so hungry, and I left my lunch at home.
   B That's OK, _____ some money. (lend)

4. A I don't know what kind of computer to buy.
   B If you want, _____ you to decide. (help)

5. A Who's going to take care of the children while I go grocery shopping?
   B _____ that, but I have to leave by 4:00. (do)

6. A I don't want to ride with you because you're never on time!
   B Don't worry. _____ (not be late)

2 A surprise party

Conversation strategies Complete the conversation with the responses in the box.

> OK. Sure. I can send invitations online. I'll do that today.
> All right. I can make one. Maybe a chocolate one?
> OK. I will. Um, maybe you can call Lynn and tell her I'm organizing her birthday party!
> Um . . . all right. I'll call and order – how many?
> ✓ OK. I have plenty of space.
> Um, all right. I'll think of something.

Nicole Tara, can we have Lynn's birthday party at your place this weekend? Mine's too small.

Tara *OK. I have plenty of space.*

Nicole And we should make a cake, but I'm not very good at baking. Can you make one?

Tara _____

Nicole That sounds good. And would you mind doing the invitations, too? You're good at that stuff.

Tara _____

Nicole And then we need a gift. Do you have any ideas? I mean, could you get her something?

Tara _____

Nicole Thanks. I'll pay you for it. Oh, and one other thing. Should we order pizza or . . . ?

Tara _____

Nicole Maybe four? Well, thanks Tara. I guess I'll go home. Call me if you need anything.

Tara _____

3 A busy weekend

Conversation strategies Respond to the requests. Then make an offer using your own ideas.

1. Could you make your special chicken dish for dinner? *All right. I'll make a salad, too.*

2. Can you help me buy a new tablet? _____

3. Could you come with me to the gym on Saturday morning? _____

4. Can you help me with my homework? _____

5. Could you help me clean the kitchen? _____

1 Print it out!

Reading | **A** Read the article. Then circle the best title.

Print Your Own Shoes   The Future of 3-D Printing   Building New Homes

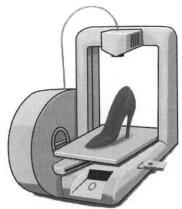

Imagine you're getting ready for a night out. First, you go online and pick out a pair of shoes. Second, you choose the size, style, and color. Next, you download the design and "print" the shoes. Finally, you put on your new shoes, and you're ready to walk out the door.

You may think that's impossible, and you might be right. There are some three-dimensional, or 3-D, printers in the world today, but you can't print out shoes quite yet. However, scientists believe 3-D printing will become common in the future.

Today, designers and engineers use 3-D printers to create high-tech models out of different materials, like plastic, metal, glass – even chocolate! They design the object in 3-D on a computer. Then a 3-D printer builds the object one layer at a time. These models help engineers test and improve designs before they make the real thing.

In the future, businesses will be able to print the real thing themselves. For example, when machines break down, companies will be able to print replacement parts and fix the machines the same day. Productivity will increase because workers won't have to wait for new parts to arrive. Another example is medical equipment. Doctors around the world will be able to simply print the items they need, and medical care will greatly improve!

As 3-D printers become more affordable, they will completely change shopping as we know it. Many scientists imagine an online marketplace where you will shop for designs. Then you will be able to print out footwear, jewelry, glasses, and other common objects in the comfort of your own home.

You might have a 3-D printer at home or work one day. What kinds of things could you print?

B Circle the correct responses to complete the sentences.

1. Printing your own shoes **will certainly / might** be possible in the future.
2. It **is / isn't** possible to use a 3-D printer to make things out of chocolate.
3. Right now, designers use 3-D printers to **make designs better / sell their designs**.
4. If companies have 3-D printers, they will be able to **test / repair** their own machines.
5. Engineers think that 3-D printers will become **more expensive / cheaper**.
6. In the future, 3-D printers **will / won't** change the way we buy personal items.

2 Life in the future

Writing **A** Read the paragraph. Add *First*, *Second*, *Next*, and *Finally* to the paragraph to list the examples. Change the punctuation.

Blog ▬ ◻ ✕

It is not easy to live in some big cities. For example, there are problems with traffic and pollution. However, 20 years from now, many of these cities may be better and cleaner. *First,* they will have better public transportation systems, and people won't need to drive cars. Also, there won't be many traffic jams or parking problems. There will be more open spaces and parks. People will be able to walk and cycle and spend time outdoors. The air will be cleaner because there will be fewer cars, and more cars will be electric. Industries will probably be cleaner and more efficient because solar power and wind power will be more popular. With these changes, big cities will be more attractive places to live.

B Write a short article about one of these topics. Use *First*, *Second*, *Next*, and *Finally* to list examples within the article.

- the ideal city of the future
- health in the future
- everyday life in the future
- the environment in the future

Unit 12 Progress chart

What can you do? Mark the boxes. ✓ = I can . . . ? = I need to review how to . . .	To review, go back to these pages in the Student's Book.
Grammar use *will*, *may*, and *might* to talk about the future.	118 and 119
use the present continuous and *going to* for the future.	118 and 119
use the simple present in clauses with *if*, *when*, *after*, and *before* to refer to the future.	121
Vocabulary name at least 8 new expressions for work, study, or life plans.	118 and 119
name at least 15 different occupations.	120 and 121
Conversation strategies use *I'll* to make offers and promises.	122 and 123
use *All right* and *OK* to agree to do something.	123
Writing use *first*, *second*, *next*, and *finally* to list ideas.	125

Illustration credits

Photo credits

Text credits

The top 500 spoken words

This is a list of the top 500 words in spoken North American English. It is based on a sample of four and a half million words of conversation from the Cambridge International Corpus. The most frequent word, *I*, is at the top of the list.

1. I	40. really	79. see
2. and	41. with	80. how
3. the	42. he	81. they're
4. you	43. one	82. kind
5. uh	44. are	83. here
6. to	45. this	84. from
7. a	46. there	85. did
8. that	47. I'm	86. something
9. it	48. all	87. too
10. of	49. if	88. more
11. yeah	50. no	89. very
12. know	51. get	90. want
13. in	52. about	91. little
14. like	53. at	92. been
15. they	54. out	93. things
16. have	55. had	94. an
17. so	56. then	95. you're
18. was	57. because	96. said
19. but	58. go	97. there's
20. is	59. up	98. I've
21. it's	60. she	99. much
22. we	61. when	100. where
23. huh	62. them	101. two
24. just	63. can	102. thing
25. oh	64. would	103. her
26. do	65. as	104. didn't
27. don't	66. me	105. other
28. that's	67. mean	106. say
29. well	68. some	107. back
30. for	69. good	108. could
31. what	70. got	109. their
32. on	71. OK	110. our
33. think	72. people	111. guess
34. right	73. now	112. yes
35. not	74. going	113. way
36. um	75. were	114. has
37. or	76. lot	115. down
38. my	77. your	116. we're
39. be	78. time	117. any

The top 500 spoken words

118. he's	161. five	204. sort
119. work	162. always	205. great
120. take	163. school	206. bad
121. even	164. look	207. we've
122. those	165. still	208. another
123. over	166. around	209. car
124. probably	167. anything	210. true
125. him	168. kids	211. whole
126. who	169. first	212. whatever
127. put	170. does	213. twenty
128. years	171. need	214. after
129. sure	172. us	215. ever
130. can't	173. should	216. find
131. pretty	174. talking	217. care
132. gonna	175. last	218. better
133. stuff	176. thought	219. hard
134. come	177. doesn't	220. haven't
135. these	178. different	221. trying
136. by	179. money	222. give
137. into	180. long	223. I'd
138. went	181. used	224. problem
139. make	182. getting	225. else
140. than	183. same	226. remember
141. year	184. four	227. might
142. three	185. every	228. again
143. which	186. new	229. pay
144. home	187. everything	230. try
145. will	188. many	231. place
146. nice	189. before	232. part
147. never	190. though	233. let
148. only	191. most	234. keep
149. his	192. tell	235. children
150. doing	193. being	236. anyway
151. cause	194. bit	237. came
152. off	195. house	238. six
153. I'll	196. also	239. family
154. maybe	197. use	240. wasn't
155. real	198. through	241. talk
156. why	199. feel	242. made
157. big	200. course	243. hundred
158. actually	201. what's	244. night
159. she's	202. old	245. call
160. day	203. done	246. saying

The top 500 spoken words

247. dollars	290. started	333. believe
248. live	291. job	334. thinking
249. away	292. says	335. funny
250. either	293. play	336. state
251. read	294. usually	337. until
252. having	295. wow	338. husband
253. far	296. exactly	339. idea
254. watch	297. took	340. name
255. week	298. few	341. seven
256. mhm	299. child	342. together
257. quite	300. thirty	343. each
258. enough	301. buy	344. hear
259. next	302. person	345. help
260. couple	303. working	346. nothing
261. own	304. half	347. parents
262. wouldn't	305. looking	348. room
263. ten	306. someone	349. today
264. interesting	307. coming	350. makes
265. am	308. eight	351. stay
266. sometimes	309. love	352. mom
267. bye	310. everybody	353. sounds
268. seems	311. able	354. change
269. heard	312. we'll	355. understand
270. goes	313. life	356. such
271. called	314. may	357. gone
272. point	315. both	358. system
273. ago	316. type	359. comes
274. while	317. end	360. thank
275. fact	318. least	361. show
276. once	319. told	362. thousand
277. seen	320. saw	363. left
278. wanted	321. college	364. friends
279. isn't	322. ones	365. class
280. start	323. almost	366. already
281. high	324. since	367. eat
282. somebody	325. days	368. small
283. let's	326. couldn't	369. boy
284. times	327. gets	370. paper
285. guy	328. guys	371. world
286. area	329. god	372. best
287. fun	330. country	373. water
288. they've	331. wait	374. myself
289. you've	332. yet	375. run

The top 500 spoken words

376. they'll	418. company	460. sorry
377. won't	419. friend	461. living
378. movie	420. set	462. drive
379. cool	421. minutes	463. outside
380. news	422. morning	464. bring
381. number	423. between	465. easy
382. man	424. music	466. stop
383. basically	425. close	467. percent
384. nine	426. leave	468. hand
385. enjoy	427. wife	469. gosh
386. bought	428. knew	470. top
387. whether	429. pick	471. cut
388. especially	430. important	472. computer
389. taking	431. ask	473. tried
390. sit	432. hour	474. gotten
391. book	433. deal	475. mind
392. fifty	434. mine	476. business
393. months	435. reason	477. anybody
394. women	436. credit	478. takes
395. month	437. dog	479. aren't
396. found	438. group	480. question
397. side	439. turn	481. rather
398. food	440. making	482. twelve
399. looks	441. American	483. phone
400. summer	442. weeks	484. program
401. hmm	443. certain	485. without
402. fine	444. less	486. moved
403. hey	445. must	487. gave
404. student	446. dad	488. yep
405. agree	447. during	489. case
406. mother	448. lived	490. looked
407. problems	449. forty	491. certainly
408. city	450. air	492. talked
409. second	451. government	493. beautiful
410. definitely	452. eighty	494. card
411. spend	453. wonderful	495. walk
412. happened	454. seem	496. married
413. hours	455. wrong	497. anymore
414. war	456. young	498. you'll
415. matter	457. places	499. middle
416. supposed	458. girl	500. tax
417. worked	459. happen	